DESPERATE DAN

SUDDENLY...

POP!

HEY! AH'M COVERED IN RUBBER. IT'S JEST LIKE A DIVER'S SUIT — JUST GREAT FOR FISHIN'.

AH'LL TAKE A RUNNIN' JUMP OFF THE END OF THE PIER!

CLUMP! CLUMP! CLUMP! CLUMP! CLUMP! CLUMP!

BUT...

ER — AH'LL TAKE A SUDDEN DROP THROUGH THE PIER INSTEAD.

KRUMP!

SNEAKER'S SLY SNEAKS

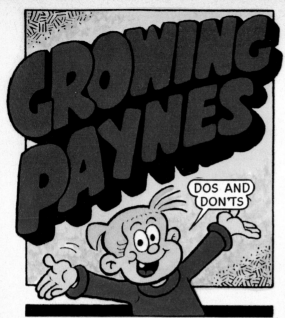

GROWING PAYNES

DOS AND DON'TS

Do get a posh pair of wellies.

Do keep money in your wellies.

Don't do handstands while you're keeping money in them!

Do play "snowploughs".

Don't play football!

Don't try to walk in them till you take the joining string off!

Do paddle in wellies.

Don't paddle too deeply!

Do fill your brother's wellies with custard.

Don't get caught!

Do get Mum to help you take them off.

DON'T push with your other foot — not if you want any supper for the next month!

Cuddles and Dimples
COO! LOOK AT ALL 'EM STARS, DIMPLES.
YEAH! 'AT'S WHERE ALLA ALIENS ANNA UFO'S COME FROM.

Marvo the WONDER CHICKEN

with HENRY THRAPPLEWHACKER the FORTYNINTH

OOK!

TARZAN CITY! THIS PLACE IS FULL OF GIANT WILD APES!

GRUNT!

GRR! WHO ARE YOU CALLING APES?

URK! THE APES ARE TURNING UGLY.

AND UGLY?

A SHARP EXIT OUT OF THE APES' TERRITORY REQUIRED.

THIS IS BRILL.

BONK! BASH! BONK!

SLAM!

PHEW! BARELY ESCAPED THOSE SAVAGES IN ONE PIECE.

AW. ME WANTS TO GO BACK IN.

GREENSVILLE! THIS IS THE REAL THING.

BOTANIC GARDENS

CRUMBS. IT'S PRETTY DARK AND CREEPY IN HERE.

OO-ER! I'M GETTING SHIVERS DOWN MY SPINE.

DRIBBLE!

A PUZZLE, FOLKS

AROUND THE WORLD WITH BULLY BEEF AND CHIPS

However —

SNEAKER'S SLY SNEAKS

ER-ATIONS!

Colonel Von Kluck's chicken farm.

IT IS EGGS THOSE CHICKS HAD BETTER BEEN LAYING, JA, BY GOLLY.

CALLING BREWSTER! COLONEL VON KLUCK APPROACHING.

PLACES EVERYONE!

GOOD MORNING, CHICKENS. SURRENDER TO ME YOUR EGGS, AT ONCE!

BY GOLLY, IT LAYS EGGS A DOZEN AT A TIME AND ALREADY PACKAGED — EVEN WITH THE BAR CODE.

OFF YOU GO, ROBOT. I WILL NOW ORDER HUNDREDS MORE.

HUSH UP, ROBOT. I'M WATCHIN' LITTLE COOP ON THE PRAIRIE.

THAT IS JUST TOO GOOD.

I NOW PRESS THE DELAY BUTTON.

CLUMP! CLUMP!

IF THEY ARE MAKING WITH DER LAUGHS AND CHUCKLES FOR THEM IT WILL NOT BE GOOD.

Uh-oh.

LAYERS AND GENTLEMEN! INTRODUCING ON THE HIGH PERCH . . .

BREWSTER ROOSTER'S — BARNYARD CIRCUS *

. . . THE AMAZING RHODE ISLAND ROXANNE!

NOT ONE EGG? YOU LAZY BIRDS HAVE GONE TOO FAR THIS TIME.

Later, that day —

ROBOTRON INC. BATTERY HEN

GOOD! MY PACKAGE HAS ARRIVED.

WITH ROBOT HENS I WILL REPLACE THOSE LAZY CHICKS.

R-R-ROBOT?

WHAT HAPPENED THERE, BREWSTER?

HEH! HEH! OL' VON KLUCK'S ROBOT OBEYS MY REMOTE CONTROL.

SPOFF!

O DE HEN LAYS DE EGGS LL OVER DE COLONEL.

HEE! HEE! THE BEST LAID PLANS DON'T ALWAYS WORK, COLONEL.

BAH! BY GOLLY.

CLUNG!

BLINKY

AWLK!

SOON HAVE THE JOB ALL TIED UP.

OUT!

BLAST!

WOW! IT WAS A HAND-DRIER. WORKS BRILL NOW.

OOPS! SORRY, MRS JONES. I'D RECOGNISE YOUR MOCK FUR COAT ANYWHERE.

MOCK FUR?

BUMP!

HOW ARE YOU FEELING AFTER YOUR COLD?

R-R-RUFF!

OH, DEAR. THAT BAD, EH?

ZE FLEE!

TERROR!

WAAA!

WHAT YOU NEED IS A SLAP-UP FEED. ALLOW ME TO TREAT YOU.

NOW YOU'RE TALKING.

CAFE

Back at the circus . . .

SNEAKER'S SLY SNEAKS

Is Dan all dried up? See the next instalment of this steamy tale of dust and disaster on Page 120.

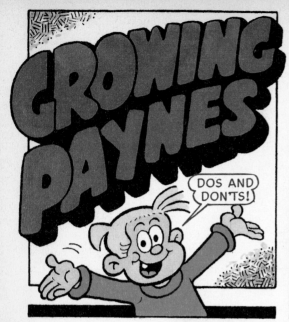

GROWING PAYNES

DOS AND DON'TS!

Do be early for school.

Do take sports' kit.

Don't take your big brother's sports' kit!

Do learn to write.

SKRREEK!

Don't forget to learn to read at the same time!

BOYS

GIRLS

Don't be too early!

RATTLE!

Do polish your shoes well.

Don't polish the soles as well!

SLIP!

Do go to school dinners.

Don't forget an emergency sandwich!

Do be in time for the bus.

BUS STOP

Don't get on the wrong one!

BERYL THE PERIL

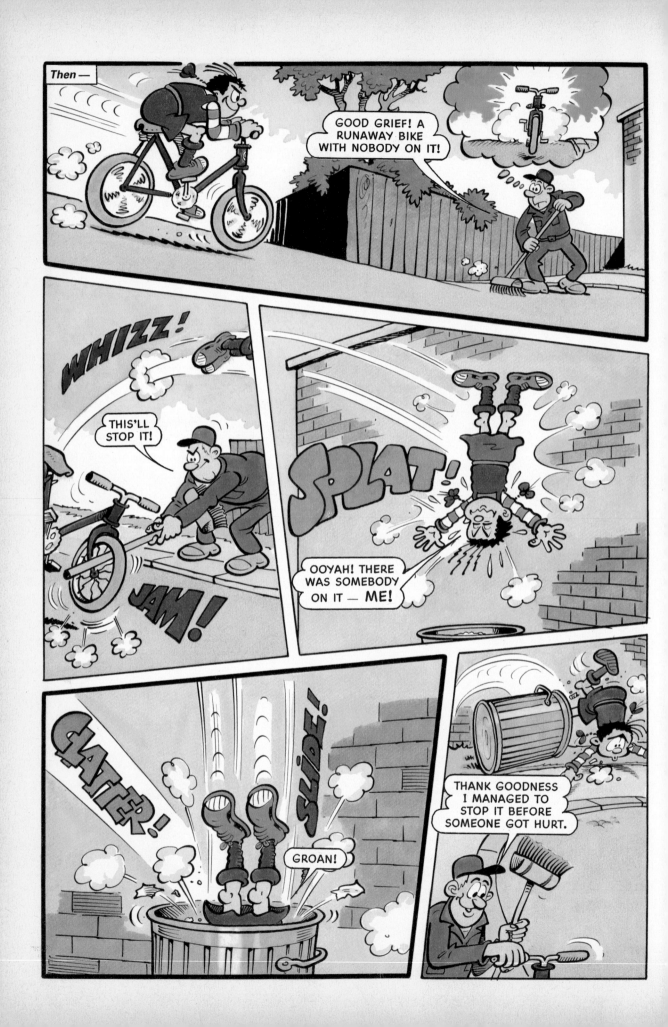

BEST COMEDY PERFORMER

MARVO THE WONDER CHICKEN

TRIP!

WE'VE GOT AN OUTING TODAY, CLASS...

GLOOM

...TO THE TOY FACTORY.

TOY FACTORY?

WITH TOYS AN' STUFF?

COOL.

WHAT ARE WE WAITIN' FOR?

WE'VE GOT AN OUTING TODAY, CLASS . . .

GLOOM

. . . TO THE TOY FACTORY.

TOY FACTORY?

WITH TOYS AN' STUFF?

COOL.

WHAT ARE WE WAITIN' FOR?

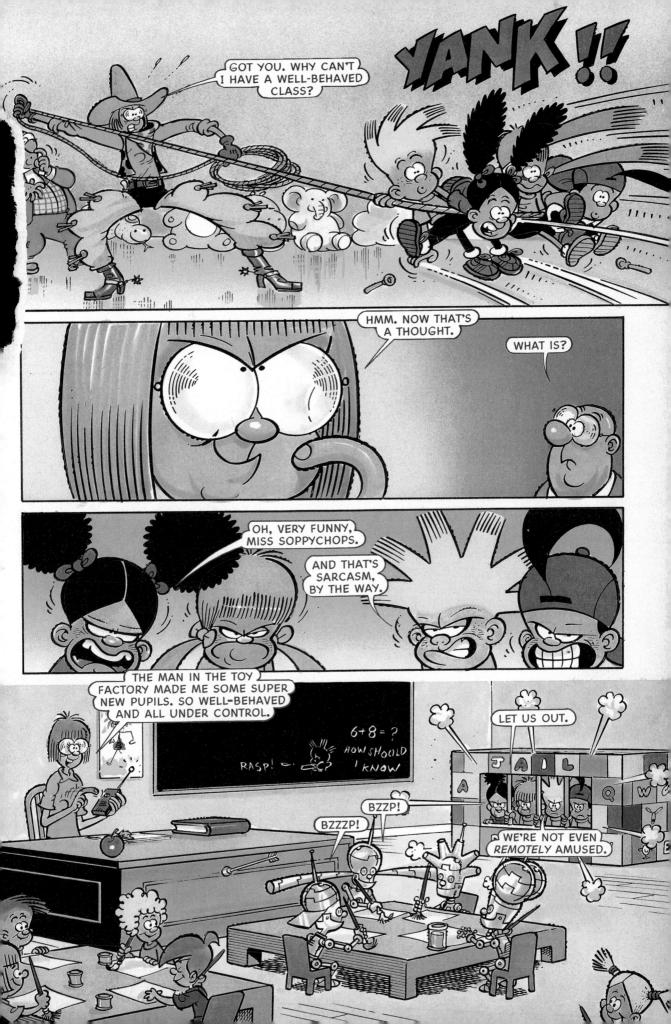

Desperate DAN in Some Like It Hot!

PART 2

In case you don't know it, Cactusville has been hit by a drought since Dan turned its water supply into a steam central-heating system.

WE CAN'T LAST MUCH LONGER WITHOUT WATER, DAN.

AH'LL LOOK FOR ANOTHER SUPPLY!

SO . . .

AH'LL NEED A FEW SUPPLIES.

THAT LOT WOULD FEED THE WHOLE TOWN FOR A MONTH.

THEN . . .

AH'LL JUST BORROW THE T.V. AERIAL, AUNT AGGIE!

EH? WHAT ON EARTH FOR?

DIVINERS FIND WATER USING THINGS LIKE THIS.

AHA! IT'S WORKING! IT'S TWITCHING!

NOW AH HEAD FOR THE HILLS.

AND SOON . . .

AH THOUGHT AH'D SHOVEL SNOW THROUGH THE PIPES DOWN TO THE LAKE — BUT IT'S TAKIN' TOO LONG.

SUDDENLY . . .

HEY! WHERE'D YOU COME FROM?

MY HIBERNATION CAVE. NOW YOU'VE WOKEN ME UP. GRR!

AH DON'T WANT TO HURT IT. AH'LL HIDE IN A SNOWDRIFT.

WHUMP!

HAW-HAW! HE'S RUN INTO A CLIFF FACE.

THE END

MARSHMALLOW

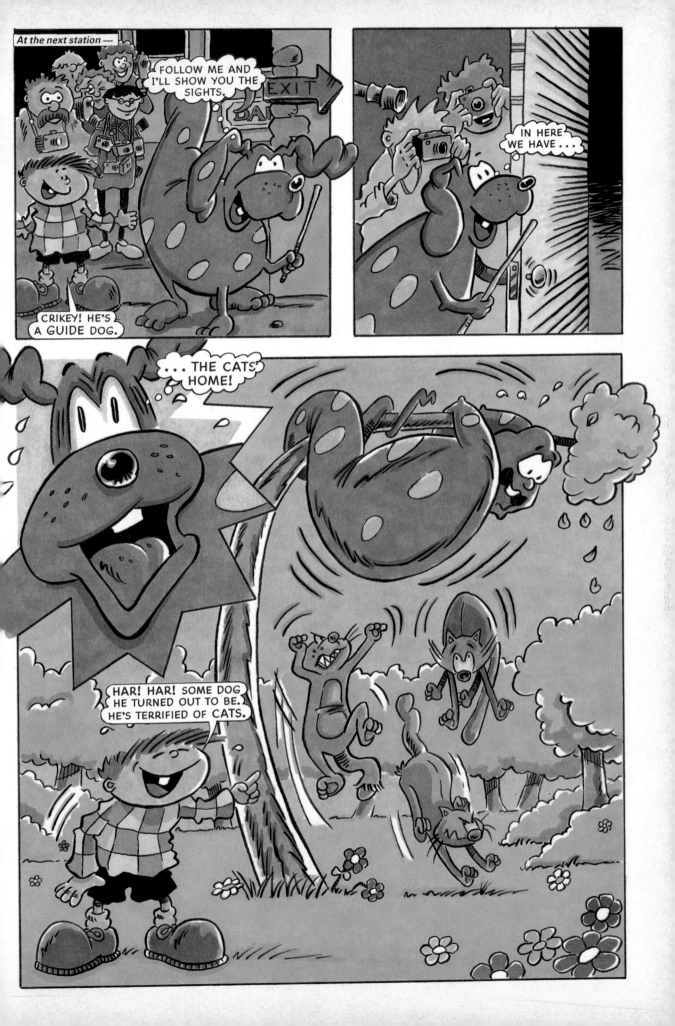

Meanwhile, inside the strange craft —

CHUCKLE! YOUR PEOPLE WILL PAY GOOD MONEY TO GET YOU BACK.

THAT ICEMAN IS A COLD-HEARTED VILLAIN!

FREEZE NOT A JOLLY GOOD FELLOW.

Just then —

I'M GOING TO TELL CHIEF O'REILLY ALL ABOUT THIS.

HEY! YOU'RE A PRICKLY CUSTOMER, AREN'T YOU?

So —

THEN THIS SPACESHIP KNOCKED ME INTO A BUSH AND —

SUCK!

SOUNDS A BIT FAR-FETCHED, ERIC.

I CAN'T BELIEVE... AARGH! LEMME GO!

ZZZT!

CHIEFY! COME BACK, SUNBEAM.

I MUST GET TO THE BOTTOM OF THIS.

WATCH THIS!

This is Eric's secret. When he eats a banana, he turns into Bananaman!

AND HERE I AM. DANDY SUPER-HERO AND ALL-ROUND GOOD GUY.

HERE I GO, DEAR READERS!

CRASH!

OOYAH!

I FORGOT I WAS STILL INSIDE THE BUILDING.

RATTLE!

RATTLE!

Printed and Published in Great Britain by D. C. THOMSON & CO., LTD.,
185 Fleet Street, London, EC4A 2HS.
© D. C. THOMSON & CO., LTD., 1999.
ISBN 0-85116-661-X.

SEE THE WORLD'S STRONGEST MAN